DATE DUE

LYNNFIELD PUBLIC LIBRARY
LYNNFIELD, MA 01940

Published by Smart Apple Media
1980 Lookout Drive, North Mankato, Minnesota 56003

Copyright © 2003 Smart Apple Media. International copyright reserved in all countries. No part of this book may be reproduced in any form without written permission from the publisher.

Photographs by Bel-Ray Company (Trish Gumina), Steve Bruhn, Corbis (Hulton-Deutsch Collection), Daimler-Chrysler Classic Archives, Icon Sports Media (Robert Beck), David Madison Sports Images, Gunter Marx Photography, Tom Myers, Spectrum Stock (Russell Burden), TimePix (Thierry Roge), Unicorn Stock Photos (Jay Foreman, Paul Murphy)

Design and production by EvansDay Design

LIBRARY OF CONGRESS CATALOGING-IN-PUBLICATION DATA

Frisch, Aaron.
Motocross / by Aaron Frisch.
p. cm. — (World of sports)
Summary: Surveys the history, equipment, techniques, risks, and safety factors of motocross, a type of motorcycle racing characterized by unpaved courses with rugged terrain, jumps, and berms.
ISBN 1-58340-164-4
1. Motocross—Juvenile literature. [1. Motocross.
2. Motorcycle racing.] I. Title. II. World of sports (North Mankato, Minn.).

GV1060.12 .F75 2002
796. 7'5—dc21 2002017710

First Edition
9 8 7 6 5 4 3 2 1

11-4-08

AARON FRISCH

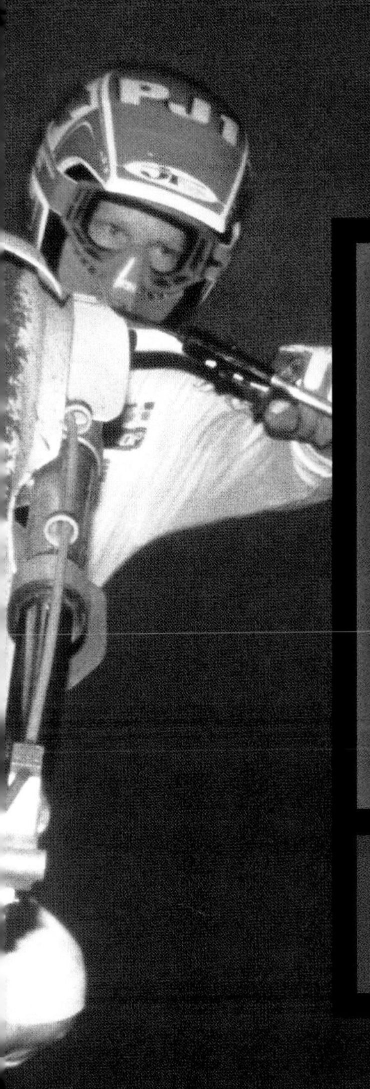

I think we've helped to establish it as the newest, gnarliest sport. We're going a lot bigger than anyone else. We're doing stuff that the BMX guys are doing, only they're doing maybe 15-foot gaps, and we've got motors so we're doing it over 80- or 100-foot gaps.

Mike Cinqmars, FREESTYLE MOTOCROSS RIDER

The History of Motocross

The air is filled with blue smoke and the whine of motorcycles as 20 riders sit side-by-side in a pack, each twisting his **throttle**. Stretching out before them is a rugged, winding track flanked by throngs of spectators. A mechanical gate in front of the riders falls, and the riders surge forward, their back tires throwing **roost** high into the air.

The first scrambles often were more about strength than skill. It was a challenge simply keeping the beastly machines upright at times, and scrambles winners often were those riders strong enough to push their bikes through mud holes ahead of the other racers.

As they fly down the track elbow-to-elbow, some riders are forced off course. Others fall and are quickly left behind. Those left upright whip through the first turn, and one part of the race is over. What remains are 40 minutes of intense speed, spectacular turns, and daredevil jumps. This is motocross, one of the most exciting motor sports in the world.

Motocross combines the thrilling acceleration and strategies of road racing with the physical demands of athletic competition. It's a sport of skill, courage, strength, and recklessness that continues to grow in

popularity in Canada and the United States. But motocross is a relatively new development in North America. In fact, the sport traces all of its roots back to Europe.

The world's first motorcycle was built in Germany in 1885. In the 1920s, British riders began gathering in meadows in the English countryside for off-road motorcycle races called "scrambles." These races were run over rugged terrain that included rocky areas, large mud holes, water crossings, and many bumps and **jumps**.

Often, the biggest challenge for the first scrambles riders was simply staying upright on their motorcycles. Because off-road cycles had not yet been developed, racers rode ponderous road motorcycles. These bikes weighed up to 400 pounds (182 kg) and had no shock-absorbing **suspension system** of any kind. Riders held on for dear life as they were bounced and jostled by the machines.

In the early 1940s, scrambles were halted because of World War II. When peace finally returned to Europe, many large racing facilities had been destroyed. All that was needed for scrambles, however, was rugged, open land, and soon off-road racing was more popular than ever.

In 1930, a Swedish motorcycle manufacturer called the Husqvarna Company began building the Specialracer Motorcykel, a bike designed specifically for scrambles. By the 1940s, scrambles had loyal followings in Britain, France, Germany, and Italy, and the term "motocross" (a combination of the French word "motocyclette" and "cross-country") came into use.

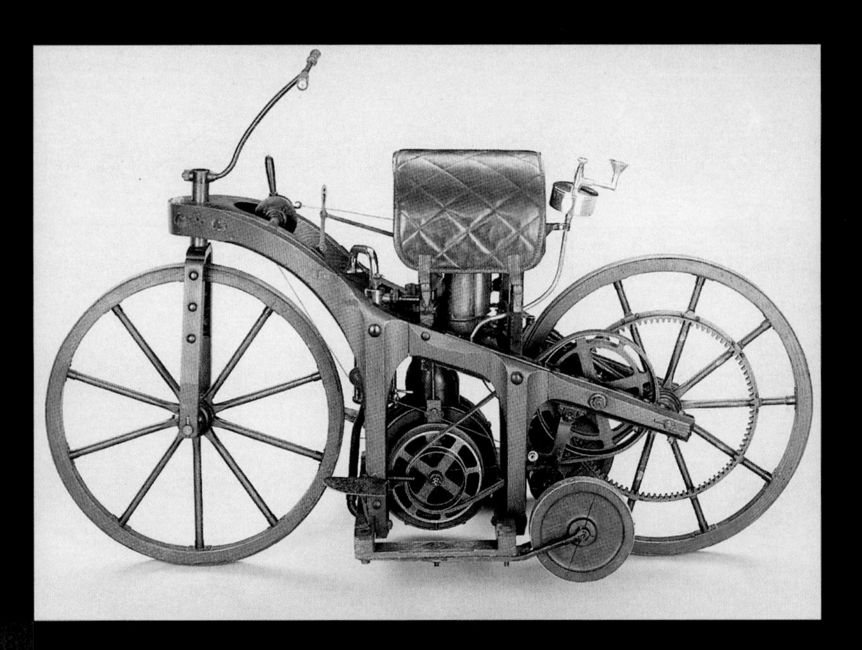

throttle *a valve that releases gas to an engine, giving a motorcycle more speed or power; it is controlled by twisting a handlebar*

roost *streams of loose dirt thrown into the air by motorcycle tires*

jumps *sizable ramps or mounds of dirt that propel riders into the air*

The world was introduced to the motorcycle in 1885 in the form of this bulky German machine.

suspension system *an arrangement of springs that connects all of a motorcycle's parts to the frame*

exhaust pipes *pipes that release the gases created by the burning of gasoline*

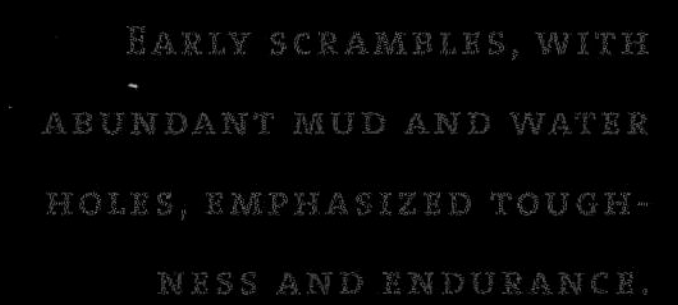

EARLY SCRAMBLES, WITH ABUNDANT MUD AND WATER HOLES, EMPHASIZED TOUGHNESS AND ENDURANCE.

As the popularity of motocross spread, British cycle manufacturers such as Norton, BSA, Triumph, and Ariel began producing lighter, more powerful motorcycles. These bikes had more comfortable seats and wider tires with big knobs for better traction on dirt. They also had stronger frames and upturned **exhaust pipes** less likely to be damaged by rocks and logs.

In 1947, a Frenchman named Roland Poirer established an international motocross competition called the "Motocross des Nations." Regulations for this groundbreaking event were set by a new organization called the Federation Internationale Motocycliste (FIM), which was created to oversee the running of motocross competitions everywhere.

Most North Americans first heard of motocross in the 1960s. In 1966, a man named M. Edison Dye began importing Husqvarna motorcycles to the United States. He also invited European motocross riders to compete in off-road races in America. By displaying correct racing form and technique, the Europeans helped motocross put down roots in North America.

Courses and Equipment

Although modern motocross courses vary from track to track, all share a number of features. They are laid out in irregular shapes and range in length from one to three miles (1.6–4.8 km). They are loaded with tight turns, steep uphill and downhill sections, and obstacles such as large rocks, ruts, and mud holes. The course boundaries often are lined with hay bales, which soften the impact of crashes.

One of the key changes made to off-road motorcycles in the 1940s was the addition of foot-controlled shift levers. Before this time, riders had to shift gears by hand, adding to the difficulty of handling the heavy bikes.

Other key features of motocross courses are jumps and berms. Jumps offer immense challenge to riders and add to the visual excitement of the races. Riders sometimes exceed speeds of 65 miles (105 km) per hour in motocross, and hitting a jump at high speeds can send them 60 feet (18 m) or more through the air. Berms, meanwhile, are mounds of dirt that build up in the corners as motorcycles slide through turns and move dirt with their back tires. They create a banked surface that allows riders to change direction quickly.

ARTS
LIMITED
ROAD CRAMPS
DCSHOECOUSA

Today, engine size is the biggest difference from one motocross motorcycle to the next. Most modern cycles have one cylinder—a long, hollow tube in the engine that houses a **piston**. When gasoline is fed from a fuel tank into the cylinder, the piston fires up and down to turn a **crankshaft**. (The two combined strokes of the piston turn the crankshaft once, which is why motocross engines are called two-stroke engines.) The area inside the cylinder is measured in cubic centimeters (cc).

Motocross took a big step forward as a major form of racing in 1952. That year, the FIM created a European motocross championship series that featured major races in several countries.

WITH ITS SMALL ENGINE AND FAIRLY LIGHT FRAME, A 125 CC MOTORCYCLE TRADES POWER FOR MANEUVERABILITY.

piston *a moving piece that fires back and forth inside a cylinder to drive an engine*

crankshaft *a rod connected to a cylinder that turns around to help drive an engine*

THE BIGGER A MOTOCROSS BIKE'S ENGINE, THE GREATER THE SPEED—AND THE BIGGER THE AIR—A RIDER CAN ATTAIN.

A bike's speed and power is determined by the size of its cylinder. The bigger the cylinder, the higher the number of cubic centimeters and the heavier and more powerful the engine. The three main classes of motocross bikes are 125 cc, 250 cc, and 500 cc. A 500 cc is five times as powerful as a 125 cc. Most motocross riders enter the sport on 125s and then move up as their strength and skill level improves.

The most popular motocross cycles in the world today are made by Japanese companies such as Honda, Suzuki, Kawasaki, and Yamaha. Bikes are as lightweight as they can be without sacrificing strength, with the average bike (a 250 cc) weighing about 230 pounds (98 kg). Attached to a motor-

FACTORY RIDERS ARE OFTEN ADORNED WITH THE NAMES OR LOGOS OF THE COMPANIES THAT SPONSOR THEM

cycle's frame is a strong suspension system, knobby tires, wide handlebars, and a high front-wheel fender.

In 1957, a German rider named Fritz Betzelbacher won the first race of the FIM's European motocross series. The win was a historic one because Betzelbacher's cycle had a two-stroke engine at a time when almost all motocross bikes had heavier four-stroke engines.

At top levels of competition, successful motocross riders may be sponsored by a major motorcycle manufacturer. These so-called "factory riders" are paid a regular salary and usually are provided with free motorcycles, equipment, and mechanical support. In return, the riders endorse the company's equipment and often wear its logo on their jersey or helmet. Riders who do not have this corpo-

LIKE SOLDIERS IN BODY ARMOR, MOTOCROSS RIDERS GEAR UP WITH AN ARRAY OF PROTECTIVE EQUIPMENT.

rate support are called "privateers" and are responsible for all of their own expenses.

Motocross riders wear extensive protective equipment any time they're on the track. This equipment includes a padded helmet, goggles, and a long-sleeved jersey worn over or under a padded chest protector. Riders wear leather pants padded at the knees and hips, as well as high leather boots, which protect the legs from the heat of a bike's engine. Leather gloves and mouth guards complete the outfit. Motocross riders can't be too careful—even a small crash can be dangerous without protective equipment.

The Motocross des Nations still takes place every year in Europe. All countries that have motocross send three of their best riders to compete. Each of the three riders competes in a different class (125 cc, 250 cc, or Open, in which any motorcycle is allowed), and the points are added up to see which country wins.

A Day at the Races

In the early days of motocross, the sport was very informal. The length of races varied from weekend to weekend, and riders usually were free to use any size bike they wanted. Because many tracks weren't formally laid out, sometimes riders would take shortcuts to reach the finish line first. It wasn't until the 1970s that the FIM and other organizations established firm rules for motocross.

Instead of sitting on the seat while riding, motocross riders often stand on the footpegs. When doing this, the rider's legs help to absorb the impact of bumps. This is often more comfortable than sitting on the seat, especially when crossing rough areas.

A day at the track for motocross racing is a busy and exciting one. Once riders arrive at the course, their bikes are prepared for the race in an area called "the pits." When the cycles are ready, riders take a few practice laps to test their bikes and get a feel for the course. Usually races are run rain or shine, so riders must be prepared for any kind of track surface.

A motocross race consists of two separate heats called "motos," each lasting up to 40 minutes. Riders compete to finish a set number of laps

WORLD OF SPORTS
MOTOCROSS

Published by Smart Apple Media
1980 Lookout Drive, North Mankato, Minnesota 56003

Copyright © 2003 Smart Apple Media. International copyright reserved in all countries. No part of this book may be reproduced in any form without written permission from the publisher.

Photographs by Bel-Ray Company (Trish Gumina), Steve Bruhn, Corbis (Hulton-Deutsch Collection), Daimler-Chrysler Classic Archives, Icon Sports Media (Robert Beck), David Madison Sports Images, Gunter Marx Photography, Tom Myers, Spectrum Stock (Russell Burden), TimePix (Thierry Roge), Unicorn Stock Photos (Jay Foreman, Paul Murphy)

Design and production by EvansDay Design

LIBRARY OF CONGRESS CATALOGING-IN-PUBLICATION DATA

Frisch, Aaron.
Motocross / by Aaron Frisch.
p. cm. — (World of sports)
Summary: Surveys the history, equipment, techniques, risks, and safety factors of motocross, a type of motorcycle racing characterized by unpaved courses with rugged terrain, jumps, and berms.
ISBN 1-58340-164-4
1. Motocross—Juvenile literature. [1. Motocross.
2. Motorcycle racing.] I. Title. II. World of sports (North Mankato, Minn.).

GV1060.12 .F75 2002
796. 7'5—dc21 2002017710

First Edition
9 8 7 6 5 4 3 2 1

MOTOCROSS

A A R O N   F R I S C H

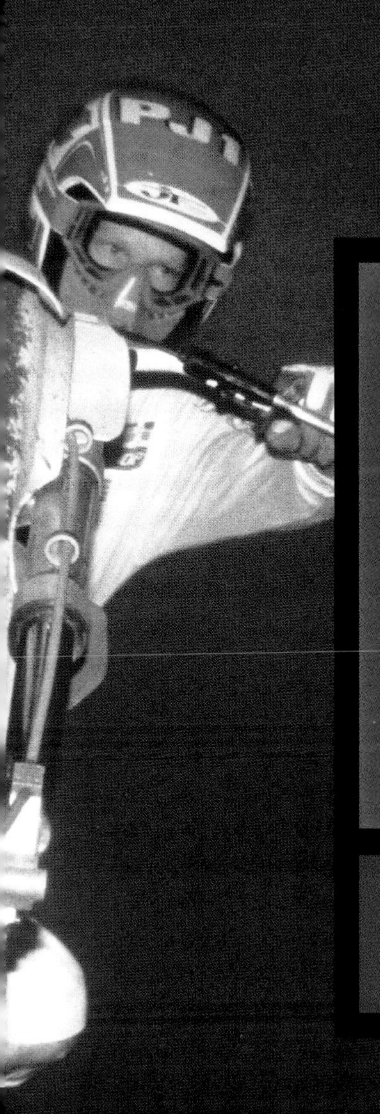

I think we've helped to establish it as the newest, gnarliest sport. We're going a lot bigger than anyone else. We're doing stuff that the BMX guys are doing, only they're doing maybe 15-foot gaps, and we've got motors so we're doing it over 80- or 100-foot gaps.

Mike Cinqmars, FREESTYLE MOTOCROSS RIDER

The History of Motocross

The air is filled with blue smoke and the whine of motorcycles as 20 riders sit side-by-side in a pack, each twisting his **throttle**. Stretching out before them is a rugged, winding track flanked by throngs of spectators. A mechanical gate in front of the riders falls, and the riders surge forward, their back tires throwing **roost** high into the air.

The first scrambles often were more about strength than skill. It was a challenge simply keeping the beastly machines upright at times, and scrambles winners often were those riders strong enough to push their bikes through mud holes ahead of the other racers.

As they fly down the track elbow-to-elbow, some riders are forced off course. Others fall and are quickly left behind. Those left upright whip through the first turn, and one part of the race is over. What remains are 40 minutes of intense speed, spectacular turns, and daredevil jumps. This is motocross, one of the most exciting motor sports in the world.

Motocross combines the thrilling acceleration and strategies of road racing with the physical demands of athletic competition. It's a sport of skill, courage, strength, and recklessness that continues to grow in

33

popularity in Canada and the United States. But motocross is a relatively new development in North America. In fact, the sport traces all of its roots back to Europe.

The world's first motorcycle was built in Germany in 1885. In the 1920s, British riders began gathering in meadows in the English countryside for off-road motorcycle races called "scrambles." These races were run over rugged terrain that included rocky areas, large mud holes, water crossings, and many bumps and **jumps**.

Often, the biggest challenge for the first scrambles riders was simply staying upright on their motorcycles. Because off-road cycles had not yet been developed, racers rode ponderous road motorcycles. These bikes weighed up to 400 pounds (182 kg) and had no shock-absorbing **suspension system** of any kind. Riders held on for dear life as they were bounced and jostled by the machines.

In the early 1940s, scrambles were halted because of World War II. When peace finally returned to Europe, many large racing facilities had been destroyed. All that was needed for scrambles, however, was rugged, open land, and soon off-road racing was more popular than ever.

In 1930, a Swedish motorcycle manufacturer called the Husqvarna Company began building the Specialracer Motorcykel, a bike designed specifically for scrambles. By the 1940s, scrambles had loyal followings in Britain, France, Germany, and Italy, and the term "motocross" (a combination of the French word "motocyclette" and "cross-country") came into use.

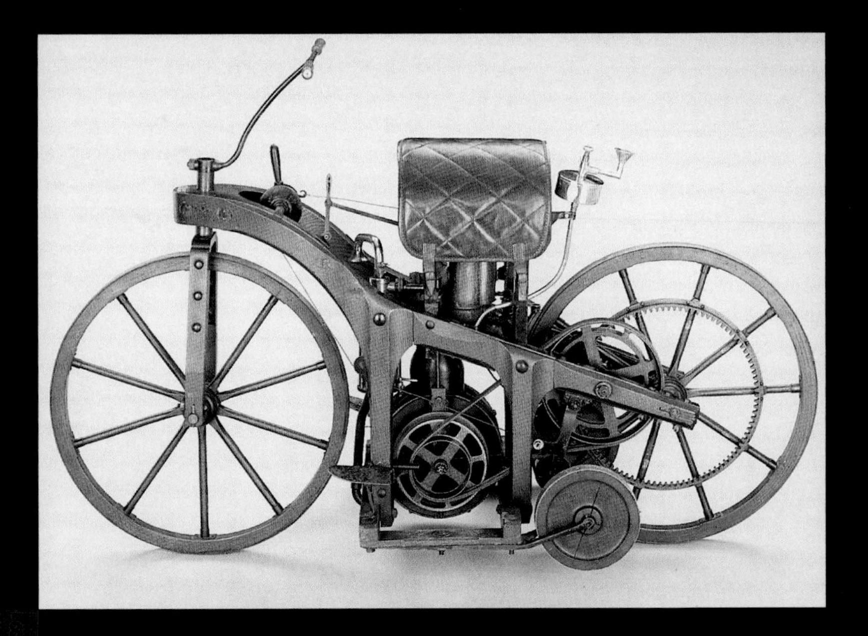

THE WORLD WAS INTRODUCED TO THE MOTORCYCLE IN 1885 IN THE FORM OF THIS BULKY GERMAN MACHINE.

throttle *a valve that releases gas to an engine, giving a motorcycle more speed or power; it is controlled by twisting a handlebar*

roost *streams of loose dirt thrown into the air by motorcycle tires*

jumps *sizable ramps or mounds of dirt that propel riders into the air*

suspension system *an arrangement of springs that connects all of a motorcycle's parts to the frame*

exhaust pipes *pipes that release the gases created by the burning of gasoline*

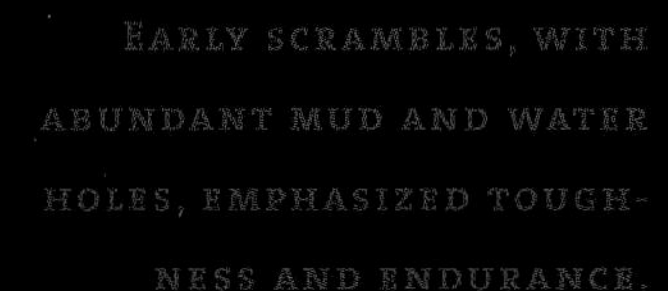

EARLY SCRAMBLES, WITH ABUNDANT MUD AND WATER HOLES, EMPHASIZED TOUGHNESS AND ENDURANCE.

As the popularity of motocross spread, British cycle manufacturers such as Norton, BSA, Triumph, and Ariel began producing lighter, more powerful motorcycles. These bikes had more comfortable seats and wider tires with big knobs for better traction on dirt. They also had stronger frames and upturned **exhaust pipes** less likely to be damaged by rocks and logs.

In 1947, a Frenchman named Roland Poirer established an international motocross competition called the "Motocross des Nations." Regulations for this groundbreaking event were set by a new organization called the Federation Internationale Motocycliste (FIM), which was created to oversee the running of motocross competitions everywhere.

Most North Americans first heard of motocross in the 1960s. In 1966, a man named M. Edison Dye began importing Husqvarna motorcycles to the United States. He also invited European motocross riders to compete in off-road races in America. By displaying correct racing form and technique, the Europeans helped motocross put down roots in North America.

Courses and Equipment

Although modern motocross courses vary from track to track, all share a number of features. They are laid out in irregular shapes and range in length from one to three miles (1.6–4.8 km). They are loaded with tight turns, steep uphill and downhill sections, and obstacles such as large rocks, ruts, and mud holes. The course boundaries often are lined with hay bales, which soften the impact of crashes.

One of the key changes made to off-road motorcycles in the 1940s was the addition of foot-controlled shift levers. Before this time, riders had to shift gears by hand, adding to the difficulty of handling the heavy bikes.

Other key features of motocross courses are jumps and berms. Jumps offer immense challenge to riders and add to the visual excitement of the races. Riders sometimes exceed speeds of 65 miles (105 km) per hour in motocross, and hitting a jump at high speeds can send them 60 feet (18 m) or more through the air. Berms, meanwhile, are mounds of dirt that build up in the corners as motorcycles slide through turns and move dirt with their back tires. They create a banked surface that allows riders to change direction quickly.

ARTS
LIMITED
DCSHOECOUSA

Today, engine size is the biggest difference from one motocross motorcycle to the next. Most modern cycles have one cylinder—a long, hollow tube in the engine that houses a **piston**. When gasoline is fed from a fuel tank into the cylinder, the piston fires up and down to turn a **crankshaft**. (The two combined strokes of the piston turn the crankshaft once, which is why motocross engines are called two-stroke engines.) The area inside the cylinder is measured in cubic centimeters (cc).

Motocross took a big step forward as a major form of racing in 1952. That year, the FIM created a European motocross championship series that featured major races in several countries.

piston *a moving piece that fires back and forth inside a cylinder to drive an engine*

crankshaft *a rod connected to a cylinder that turns around to help drive an engine*

WITH ITS SMALL ENGINE AND FAIRLY LIGHT FRAME, A 125 CC MOTORCYCLE TRADES POWER FOR MANEUVERABILITY.

THE BIGGER A MOTOCROSS BIKE'S ENGINE, THE GREATER THE SPEED—AND THE BIGGER THE AIR—A RIDER CAN ATTAIN.

A bike's speed and power is determined by the size of its cylinder. The bigger the cylinder, the higher the number of cubic centimeters and the heavier and more powerful the engine. The three main classes of motocross bikes are 125 cc, 250 cc, and 500 cc. A 500 cc is five times as powerful as a 125 cc. Most motocross riders enter the sport on 125s and then move up as their strength and skill level improves.

The most popular motocross cycles in the world today are made by Japanese companies such as Honda, Suzuki, Kawasaki, and Yamaha. Bikes are as lightweight as they can be without sacrificing strength, with the average bike (a 250 cc) weighing about 230 pounds (98 kg). Attached to a motor-

FACTORY RIDERS ARE OFTEN ADORNED WITH THE NAMES OR LOGOS OF THE COMPANIES THAT SPONSOR THEM.

cycle's frame is a strong suspension system, knobby tires, wide handlebars, and a high front-wheel fender.

In 1957, a German rider named Fritz Betzelbacher won the first race of the FIM's European motocross series. The win was a historic one because Betzelbacher's cycle had a two-stroke engine at a time when almost all motocross bikes had heavier four-stroke engines.

At top levels of competition, successful motocross riders may be sponsored by a major motorcycle manufacturer. These so-called "factory riders" are paid a regular salary and usually are provided with free motorcycles, equipment, and mechanical support. In return, the riders endorse the company's equipment and often wear its logo on their jersey or helmet. Riders who do not have this corpo-

LIKE SOLDIERS IN BODY ARMOR, MOTOCROSS RIDERS GEAR UP WITH AN ARRAY OF PROTECTIVE EQUIPMENT.

rate support are called "privateers" and are responsible for all of their own expenses.

Motocross riders wear extensive protective equipment any time they're on the track. This equipment includes a padded helmet, goggles, and a long-sleeved jersey worn over or under a padded chest protector. Riders wear leather pants padded at the knees and hips, as well as high leather boots, which protect the legs from the heat of a bike's engine. Leather gloves and mouth guards complete the outfit. Motocross riders can't be too careful—even a small crash can be dangerous without protective equipment.

The Motocross des Nations still takes place every year in Europe. All countries that have motocross send three of their best riders to compete. Each of the three riders competes in a different class (125 cc, 250 cc, or Open, in which any motorcycle is allowed), and the points are added up to see which country wins.

A Day at the Races

In the early days of motocross, the sport was very informal. The length of races varied from weekend to weekend, and riders usually were free to use any size bike they wanted. Because many tracks weren't formally laid out, sometimes riders would take shortcuts to reach the finish line first. It wasn't until the 1970s that the FIM and other organizations established firm rules for motocross.

Instead of sitting on the seat while riding, motocross riders often stand on the footpegs. When doing this, the rider's legs help to absorb the impact of bumps. This is often more comfortable than sitting on the seat, especially when crossing rough areas.

A day at the track for motocross racing is a busy and exciting one. Once riders arrive at the course, their bikes are prepared for the race in an area called "the pits." When the cycles are ready, riders take a few practice laps to test their bikes and get a feel for the course. Usually races are run rain or shine, so riders must be prepared for any kind of track surface.

A motocross race consists of two separate heats called "motos," each lasting up to 40 minutes. Riders compete to finish a set number of laps

LYNNFIELD PUBLIC LIBRARY
LYNNFIELD, MA 01940